CREATURES
at My Feet

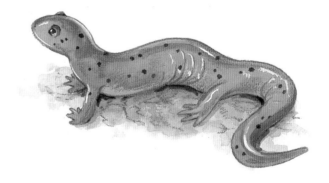

CREATURES
at My Feet

by Sherry Neidigh
with text by Charles E. Davis

rising moon

Books for Young Readers from Northland Publishing

www.northlandpub.com

FIRST EDITION, 1993
First Paperback Edition, July 1999
Second Printing, May 2000
ISBN 0-87358-739-1

Library of Congress Cataloging-in-Publication Data

Neidigh, Sherry.
Creatures at my feet / by Sherry Neidigh ; with text by
Charles E. Davis. — 1st ed.
p.   cm.
Summary: Describes in rhyme the animals that one can
see at ground level, such as turtles, crabs, and lizards.
1. Animals—Juvenile poetry. 2. Children's poetry, American.
[1. Animals—Poetry. 2. American poetry.] I. Davis, Charles E.,
date.   II. Title.
PS3564.E285C74   1993
811'.54—dc20   92-82135

239/2.4M/5-00

To my mother and father, for putting up with a temperamental artist after all these years.

—S.N.

To my children, Drex, McKane, McKenzie, and Merek, who are constantly revealing the world and its wonders to their most attentive students—their mother and me.

—C.E.D.

Creatures almost everywhere—
on land, in space, at sea.
You'll spy the creatures at my feet
as you follow me.

The forest is alive with things—
you'll see them everywhere.
In fact, to keep from hurting them,
you have to walk with care.

A beach is such a special place,
just made for you and me,
and with the sand and waves we'll find
small creatures from the sea.

The desert lands are dry and hot.
It seems that nothing's there,
but lizards, snakes, spiders, and bugs
hide nearly everywhere.

The snows of winter rest upon
some creatures while they sleep,
but if we watch, we'll see a few
that like to hop and peep.

The meadow in the springtime stirs
from underneath the snow.
Its creatures wake and stretch and sing
to give us all a show.

In Spencer's pond strange creatures swim
around my feet and toes.
I wonder if these creatures think
my big toe is my nose?

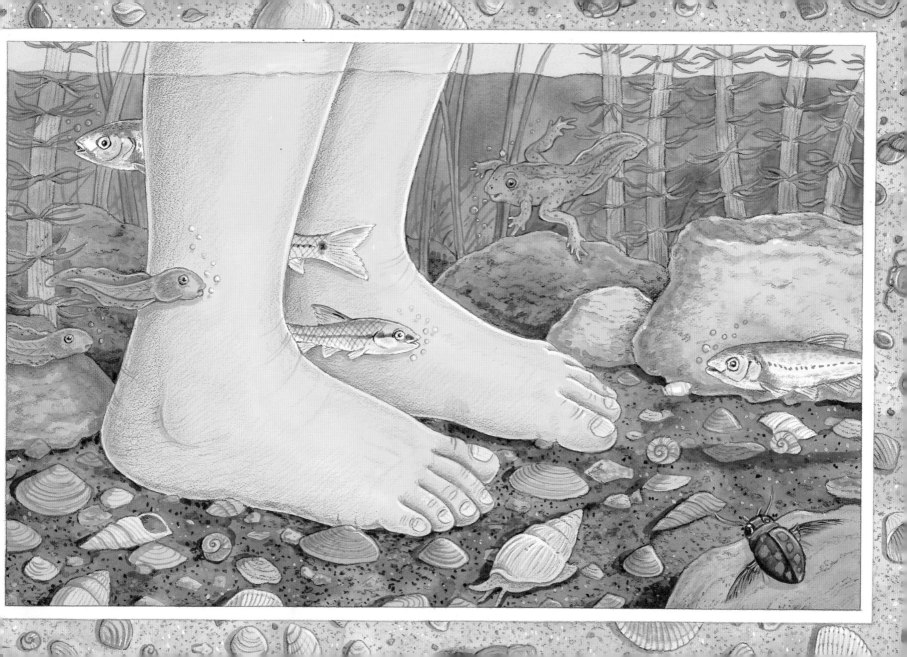

A farm has many things to see:
the horses, cows, and wheat.
The things that I like best of all
are creatures at my feet.

Cities of cement and steel
have cars on every street,
and creatures here will make a home
right under people's feet.

I love a park with deep, green grass
where everyone has fun.
Creatures even come, I think,
to picnic and to run.

On Mars the creatures that I find
are covered with green hair.
They say it comes from never having
had a breath of air.

You've seen so many creatures as
they fly, crawl, swim, or creep.
You may be ready now for bed,
so close your eyes and sleep.

But just before you snuggle up
and pull your covers tight,
look down and give the creatures in
your room a warm "Good night."

About the Illustrator

SHERRY NEIDIGH said she created the concept of *Creatures at My Feet* "because my grandmother always said I liked to rearrange the ants on the sidewalk when I was a kid." She is an award-winning artist and graphic designer whose experience includes designing toys for Hallmark Cards and working with a pediatrics ward in a Phoenix, Arizona hospital to create orientation materials for children.

Currently, Sherry is a freelance illustrator living in Charlotte, North Carolina, with a sheltie dog named Basil Knawbone, who likes to be at her feet.

About the Author

CHARLES E. DAVIS has published a number of his stories in leading magazines for children and young adults. He is currently working on a sequel to his novel for young adults *The Great Chase* (Covenant Communications). An attorney, Charlie is one of the founders of the internet site law.com, and is also the author of a number of business- and law-related articles and books.

Charlie lives with his wife, four children, and a wall of children's books in Mesa, Arizona. You can write to him at charlie@law.com.

Can you find these animals in this book?

Ant
Beetle
Butterfly
Caterpillar
Chicken
Chipmunk
Crab
Duck
Fish
Frog
Honeybee
Ladybug

Lizard
Mouse
Pig
Puppy
Rabbit
Rat
Sand dollar
Snail
Tadpole
Tarantula
Worm

Literacy First

PARKWAY
Title 1